SINCERITY FOREVER

Mac Wellman

BROADWAY PLAY PUBLISHING INC
224 E 62nd St, NY, NY 10065
www.broadwayplaypub.com
info@broadwayplaypub.com

SINCERITY FOREVER
© Copyright 1991 by Mac Wellman

All rights reserved. This work is fully protected under the copyright laws of the United States of America.
No part of this publication may be photocopied, reproduced, stored in a retrieval system, or transmitted, in any form or by any means, electronic, mechanical, recording, or otherwise, without the prior permission of the publisher. Additional copies of this play are available from the publisher.

Written permission is required for live performance of any sort. This includes readings, cuttings, scenes, and excerpts. For amateur and stock performances, please contact Broadway Play Publishing Inc. For all other rights contact Buddy Thomas, I C M, 40 W 57, NY NY 10019.

First printing: Dec 2005, second printing: Nov 2009
I S B N: 978-0-88145-274-7

Book design: Marie Donovan
Word processing: Microsoft Word
Typographic controls: Xerox Ventura Publisher 2.0 P E
Typeface: Palatino
Printed and bound in the U S A

SINCERITY FOREVER was first produced as the winner of the first Berkshire Theater Festival Roger Nathan Hirschl Playwriting Award. The play premiered in July 1990 at the Festival's Unicorn Theater with the following cast and creative conributors:

>LuAnn Adams
>Ariane Brandt
>Jason Duchin
>Kate Forbes
>Tom Hildreth
>Ntare Mwine
>Angie Phillips
>Tom Simpson
>Mark Singale

Director .... Richard Caliban
Music composition .... David Van Tieghem
Sets .... James Youmans
Costumes .... Mary Myers
Lighting .... Kenneth Posner

SINCERITY FOREVER was then dedicated to Senator Jesse Helms: "...for the fine job you are doing of destroying civil liberties in These States."

SINCERITY FOREVER was then produced by House Frau, Inc in November and December 1990 at Brooklyn Arts and Cultural Association (BACA) Downtown as part of the 1990 Fringe Series. The cast and creative contributors were:

>Amy Brenneman
>Frank Deal
>Zach Grenier
>Jan Harding
>Patrick Kerr
>Steve Mellor
>Dan Moran
>Leslie Nipkow
>Kenya Scott
>David Van Tieghem

Director .... Jim Simpson
Music composition .... David Van Tieghem
Set & light design .... Kyle Chepulis
Costume design .... Claudia Brown

SINCERITY FOREVER received a *Village Voice* Obie for Playwrighting in 1991.

SINCERITY FOREVER was made possible by generous support of the National Endowment for the Arts*, New York Foundation for the Arts, the John Simon Guggenheim Foundation, and is the first flower of the Roger Nathan Hirschl Playwriting Award.

*See Author's Note and Correction.

AUTHOR'S NOTE AND CORRECTION

The National Endowment for the Arts has requested that I remove credit to them for my play SINCERITY FOREVER, although I received a 1990 Playwriting Fellowship. Accordingly, the author would like to amend the error of his ways: I was wrong, SINCERITY FOREVER was not made possible by the generous assistance of the N E A. I don't know what I was thinking...
Mac Wellman, September 30, 1990

CHARACTERS

JUDY, *a sincere young person and member of the Invisible Nation*
MOLLY, *ditto*
TOM, *ditto*
HANK, *ditto*
GEORGE, *ditto*
LLOYD, *ditto*
MELVIN, *ditto*
TWO FURBALLS, *of the tribe of Belial and Abaddon*
JESUS H CHRIST, *a young African-American woman who carries a very heavy suitcase*

The occasional appearance of an asterisk (*) in the middle of a speech is used by the playwright to indicate that the next speech begins to overlap at that point. A double asterisk (**) indicates that a later speech (not the one immediately following) begins to overlap at that point. The overlapping speeches are all clearly marked in the text.

Dogs bark at a person whom they do not know.
Heraclitus

This one's for Jesse and the Wildman

Scene One

(A beautiful summer's night in the outskirts of Hillsbottom. Two girls in a parked car talking about things. Both are dressed in Ku Klux Klan garb.)

JUDY: Molly, do you know why God created the world the way he did? so complicated, I mean.

(Pause)

MOLLY: Nope.

JUDY: Because I've been thinking about it, and I just get more and more puzzled.

MOLLY: So do I.

JUDY: Because if there is a divine plan it sure doesn't look it, very divine, that is, or planlike. It looks kinda like a mess.

MOLLY: Most of the time, when I think about big things, things like God, and the end of nature, and global warming, and so on, I feel like I don't know anything at all.

JUDY: That's just how I feel. Like I don't know anything. It's really scary. I mean I don't know the name of the state capital. I don't know what my dad does at work. I couldn't name more than two or three South American countries, and I'm not much better when it comes to Europe.

MOLLY: I don't know the difference between good art and bad art. I haven't a clue what a "hostile takeover" is, nor why junk bonds are junky. I mean why would anybody want them if they're worthless? It doesn't make any sense.

JUDY: I don't know why the sky is blue, and I don't know what "blue" is, and I don't know why I don't know. *(Pause)* I don't know anything. I mean, when you come right down to it, I don't know a blessed thing, and you know? I don't care, I don't care that I don't know anything because I strongly suspect that nobody else knows anything either.

MOLLY: You think they're just pretending?

JUDY: I think they're all faking it, particularly our parents, our teachers, our social betters, people in positions of authority, and celebrities on T V, and in the halls of Congress, in the churches and klonvocations, and on the radio, even in the middle of the night when we are all asleep, except Poky the cat. Poky the cat knows. *(Long pause)* Sometimes I wonder if I'm really named Judy, and that freaks me out, because if I am not then who am I, and if I don't have a real name what am I? Maybe I don't exist and this is some kind of a cruel joke my family is playing on me, and I wouldn't put it past them, particularly Dexter, my brother. He says he has a crush on you. But I don't know if Dexter's capable of such a thing, he's such a klutz he couldn't spell I Q if you spotted him on the "Q," and he doesn't know much of anything, any more than I do. I know that for a fact.

MOLLY: Judy, I think probably God has a plan for all things, and I think the proof of this plan is in the pudding. I mean, why else would we not know anything, unless there were an intelligent being out there, somewhere, whose cunning idea it was that you and I, Judy and Molly, should be forever ignorant of the true nature of things, ignorant forever in absolute sincerity. Does Dexter really have a crush on me, or did he just say he did?

JUDY: I think the absolute sincerity part of it is the most important, because it's real hard not to know anything unless you are perfectly sincere about it. I can't remember whether he told me had this crush on you, or I just dreamed it up, or came to that conclusion because he asked what your name was.

MOLLY: I think there is this mystic furball that has infected the whole town with its poison of ignorance, and that's why none of us knows anything. And this mystic furball must be found and destroyed.

JUDY: What's a mystic furball?

MOLLY: I don't think I can explain.

JUDY: How could it make us not know anything?

MOLLY: I don't know.

JUDY: Then why did you say it did?

MOLLY: That it did what?

JUDY: You know. Make us dumb.

MOLLY: It didn't make us dumb. It made us ignorant. They aren't the same.

JUDY: But how did it do this?

MOLLY: How do I know? It was just an idea, a shot in the dark, you don't have to get so worked up about it all, you know.

JUDY: Sorry.

MOLLY: Judy.

JUDY: Yes, what is it?

MOLLY: What if, maybe , I only think I'm Molly and that in fact I'm Judy and you're Molly and that somehow we all got mixed up, tragically, walking back from school, and the mystic furball did it to us to prevent us from finding his hiding place out in the backyard, or behind the garage, or under the pile of dead leaves beside the doghouse, or behind the elm tree, or up on the roof above the dormers, or on the weather vane on top of the barn, over there, Mr. Whatsisname's barn, or deep in the ground, where the standpipes are, where we're not supposed to go, near the toxic waste dump site, where some pretty creepy stuff is supposed to be leaching into the subsoil and will eventually contaminate the groundwater and all the people for miles around will have to go around in plastic bags, on tippy toes.

JUDY: What makes you think you know all this stuff?

MOLLY: I don't.

JUDY: Then why did you say it?

MOLLY: Overheard someone at school. Guess I got carried away.

JUDY: But who said it?

MOLLY: Who said what?

JUDY: The stuff about the furball?

MOLLY: George, or Lloyd. You know, the gawky string-bean guy, the guy who said he pissed on a skunk.

JUDY: That was Lloyd, not George.

MOLLY: That's what I said.

JUDY: That's not what you said.

MOLLY: That is too.

JUDY: That is not.

MOLLY: But the most important thing is not what you know, but whether you're sincere or not. That's what I think.

JUDY: That's what I think too. If I don't know anything else I know that. I think...

MOLLY: Sincerity forever.

JUDY: Right.

(Blackout)

Scene Two

(Two guys sitting in another car. Talking. They also are decked out in Klan garb. Nice night, moon, bugs. A woman with a heavy suitcase approaches, but stands off a bit in the bushes, unseen. This is JESUS H CHRIST. *She holds a long, black staff.)*

TOM: Hank, you're so fucking dumb, you're as dumb as the north end of something headed south. Something kinda all time monster stupid.

HANK: Guess I am. But shit, you don't know much of anything yourself, Tom. You got to admit. When it comes right down to it.

TOM: Hank, you're right about that. But I got sincerity. You, you don't have no sincerity. Plus, you don't know nothing. That's a heavy weight to bear.

HANK: I always was a devious son-of-a-bitch. So I guess you're right. The way I look at it, this is the hollow time of humanity. It don't matter if we don't know nothing, because we are looking for an event, an event that will change all this weirdness, all this mediocre everydayness into something higher. Meaningful. And transcendent. Just because I was never good at chemistry or economics, or algebra, and flunked out of Hillsbottom Junior College don't mean moosedick. It don't mean moosedick because I have a special thing inside my head, here, under this pointy hat. And this thing which I'm referring to is my infinitely precious human soul, which is worth more than knowledge, because what you know is subject to the corrosive work of time, dry rot, entropy, alien juju, and the works of those who fear not God and all his works, through the malign agency of the devil who labors in the fiery furnace of hell, knitting together the warp and woof of human delusion. And that ain't beanbag.

TOM: I say a skunk is a skunk is a skunk and he ought to be rooted up, and took out and shot, and left to rot by the side of the road. You're not talking normal, Hank.

HANK: I say that I worry a lot about things like nontemporal accountability and infinite regress and the fiery pit. I worry a lot about hell, and where it is, and what it looks like, and who lives there, and who receives which torment, and what these torments feel like, since if I was capable of feeling the true nature of these torments for even the fraction of a second I might know how to amend the howling madness of my ways, even though I'd most like remain for sure an ignorant cuss and not worth a crap in the scale of things, not worth a mote in the eye of the least of the angels in the radiant economy of heaven. *(Pause. Looks puzzled)* Now, what the hell was it I was driving at?

TOM: You were saying you would sure bust your ass to amend the error of your ways.

HANK: That's it, that's what I would do, take up my load and run with it till, till I find someplace where I could dump it down, where it would be safe, and I would be free of these insane dreams of fur...fur and furrrrrrr...

TOM: Fur?

HANK: Fur, and furballs.

(Pause)

TOM: Hank, there's something the matter with you. Something not right, something wrong inside your head, with your brain.

HANK: I am John Q Fedup is what is wrong with me. I got a whole lot of lead weights bearing down on me, inside my head, under this pointy cloak. You couldn't imagine what it's like having this infernal thing inside you, this damned, eternal, Christian soul. This life sentence for eternity, which I never asked for, because like I said, I confess to not knowing a damn thing, nor the subtle ramifications of this not knowing, because all such knowing is as bad as knowing, and I would rather be rid of both than go to heaven even, which is my dark secret and a bad thought, but it's the truth, so help me God. I mean, why is this heaven any better than hell? I mean, really, *why!?* I don't mean to be a wiseass, I'm just curious, that's all.

(Pause)

TOM: Hank, you're a snake is what you are, a viper. Here you sit, wearing your human flesh, wearing the cloth of creation * and you dare...

JESUS: Pardon me.

TOM: Pardon me, ma'am. We are having a little conversation. *(He continues talking with* HANK.*)* The garment of flesh which the good Lord bequeathed unto you, and you find nothing better in your heart than to soil it with this doubt, this badass cynicism. No wonder you say you don't know nothing. Now. Now me, I too, may be as dumb as a post, and unclear about the multiplication table, the boundaries of more than a half dozen states, and unable to repair my own toilet, but dammit, Hank, if the English language was good enough for Jesus H. Christ then it's good enough for me. Furthermore, I do not feel compelled by reason to accept this theory of evolution, nor the periodic table of elements, nor the theory of global warming, nor the supposed crimes against the Jews attributed to one Rudolf Hitler. Nor the spherical nature of the earth, because it's against the law of nature and we would fall off for sure and my motto is: never explain, never apologize. As for the dead, they got no rights. So, I too am John Q Fedup, and we'll both have a heap of company, in this regard, in the happy land to come. Or the other place, which is where your soul, sure as hell, shall end up if you don't get a hold on yourself and cut out this bonehead crap and act normal like a man should and just get on with it. Now what can I do for you, stranger?

(Pause. JESUS puts down her heavy bag and the earth trembles. Pause.)

JESUS: This wouldn't be the town of Hillsbottom, would it?

TOM: It might be, and then it might not be.

HANK: What do you got in that there weighty box?

JESUS: Weaseldervishbullcrushing machinery.

HANK: She's crazy.

JESUS: You want to answer my question, Bud?

TOM: Go fuck yourself.

JESUS: You amaze me, gentlemen. Even though, even though nothing that was, was done did without my sayso it seems like nobody roundabout here don't know it, and that's a fact. You set there, in that wreck of a Ford, smiling like you just ate a five-hundred-pound canary, when you are in a perilous state. That's right, because there is a furball in Hillsbottom. I can detect it with my apparatus. Maybe even two. I cannot only detect 'em with my apparatus, I am able to destroy 'em with my mind, because this furball is no ordinary furball, no, it am a mystic furball, nay a monster furball, of the tribe of Abaddon and Belial, and are therefore a spirit of negation, and this furball don't give a crap whether you cling to the angel of you ignorance, this furball am bodacious and am like to bust down boundaries between things, things dear to you, and this despite the innocence of your down-home cracker ignorance, because this time ignorance won't save you as it used to was in the pretty times done did, so many times afore, during the Season of Dread and the Season of Bloating, when the mighty leviathan *(Pause)*. But I see you gentlemen are not taking this serious, as you should. I see you are mocking me, in your heart, with your vileness and pride and lust and superstition and greed and moron stupefaction, and I feel had. I feel like a loyal lover who has been rejected, and who has wearied of the object of her love, and therefore feels a disappointment. Do you know what hell is like? For I have been to the place, and know what it looks like.

TOM: Yeah, you've been to hell, and my name is Edsel Ford.

JESUS: Surely, I have been to hell and know the place, for it was I who caused it to be riven.

(Her staff turns into a snake. She begins to go offstage.)

HANK: Oh yeah, what does it look like?

JESUS: Hell looks very much like Hillsbottom.

(She goes out. Pause. They laugh.)

Scene Three

(Another wonderful night, but strange. Two lovers in a parked car. They, too, are arrayed in the Klan way. In the bushes a FURBALL *spies upon them.)*

JUDY: Do you believe that terrible things always have to happen, or not? I mean, if it's possible for some really gross and disgusting event to happen, do you think it has to, or not, which?

GEORGE: Never really thought about it.

JUDY: Neither did I, until right now.

GEORGE: The way I look at it, we must all have a purpose, a purpose that God keeps hidden from us.

JUDY: How do you mean?

GEORGE: Well, if God informed us upfront of why we were put on earth there wouldn't be any surprises in it. God must have felt he needed to liven things up, by keeping the true purpose of all this hidden. Secret, and stuff.

JUDY: Sometimes, I do wish He had made it a little clearer, though. I mean like with car crashes. Child abuse. The divorce rate, and stuff. The sacred and mystical rights of the unborn. Like the plutonium seepage problem near West Hillsbottom, all those people downwind with growths, and how you're not supposed to drink the well water in East Hillsbottom, and stuff.

GEORGE: That's not been proven.

JUDY: That's not proven, but it's suspicious. People say it is very likely a big worry.

GEORGE: It has not been scientifically proven, otherwise those in charge of the facility would come out and say so. This is not a case of God's will being murky or his plan for us, it is just a case of the evidence not being all in.

JUDY: if the evidence were all in, would it make any difference, as far as God's will goes? That's what I mean.

GEORGE: I don't think so, because nuclear pollution might still be a part of God's design, I mean his plan for Hillsbottom. We might not be able to fathom that plan, is all.

JUDY: Then we're better off not knowing that plan.

GEORGE: That's a deep thought. I think you have a deep mind, Judy.

JUDY: George, I feel so reverent when I think of all the things I don't know, and how majestic the summer sky is at night, and how much God must love us, how much he must have cared all along, millions of years ago, before he had any idea that you or I might exist.

GEORGE: You know, I've been thinking about you all week.

JUDY: I didn't think you liked me.

GEORGE: I told Carol I had a crush on you, and I'd kill her if she told anyone.

JUDY: I can't believe it. I thought I was the one with the crush.

GEORGE: I thought you thought I wasn't part of the "in" crowd.

JUDY: I can't stand those guys. They're such snobs. I can't stand conceited people.

GEORGE: Neither can I. People who think they're better than you, just because they drive a Corvette their father gave them. Like Ralph.

JUDY: I can't stand that.

GEORGE: But you went out with Ralph for six months.

JUDY: Even then I couldn't stand that about him. First I had a crush on him because I thought he was cute and stuff. But pretty soon I wised up and realized he wasn't sincere. Actually he was a jerk, and just did things to impress his friends. Like Chainsaw and Dragonwagon. Gross. And the furball guy. Whatsisname. Actually I only went out with him because he drove a red Corvette. Red's my favorite color.

GEORGE: I thought you were madly in love with him.

JUDY: I wasn't.

GEORGE: Are you sure?

JUDY: What are you talking about? You're the one who was making googly eyes all over Susan Hanahan all during the field trip to the...museum. Was it the museum?

GEORGE: No, it was the nuclear power plant. It was in the cooling unit.

JUDY: Well, you were the one who * was making eyes at her.

GEORGE: I was not making eyes at Susan Hanahan. I was only trying to make sure she had someone who could give her the lowdown on who to hang out with. I did not find her attractive. I found her pathetic, actually. But that was before I realized she had this crush on that slob Randolph. Can you believe it?

JUDY: I still cannot believe that. I still cannot believe that anyone could possibly have a crush on someone so nerdy and insincere as Randolph.

GEORGE: It's bad enough to be nerdy and insincere, but to be nerdy and insincere like Randolph is enough to make a person positively gag.

(Pause)

JUDY: I have a crush on you.

GEORGE: I have a monster crush on you.

(They laugh.)

JUDY: I didn't think anything like this would happen. I just thought you were doing me a favor because my friends aren't as cool as your friends.

GEORGE: Your friends are just as cool as my friends. I figured you might not go out with me, well, on account of how I don't know anything, and your dad being this famous pervert and all and socially unacceptable and stuff, not that any of it means moosedick to me, hell, my whole family went bankrupt and stuff. We aren't exactly the country club set.

JUDY: George, I don't care about what all those snobs think. I think you're a very sincere person, and that is the most important to me.

GEORGE: Really, Judy?

JUDY: Yes, George, it is.

GEORGE: I've never felt this good before.

JUDY: Neither have I. It's really wonderful. *(Pause)* Do you believe in God, George?

GEORGE: I didn't used to think I did, but when I think about us, and all the terrific feelings I have for you, then I think there must be a God, a god who has arranged for everything to work out perfectly, the way it should.

JUDY: I feel that way too. I feel very sure that you will accomplish wonderful things in your life, George, and that you will go to heaven.

GEORGE: I don't know, Judy, sometimes I feel I'm not up to life's challenges.

JUDY: Just because you've had some rough times doesn't mean you won't be up to the challenges of life. I think you've been very brave. And your dad was really looked up at, that's what my mom said. And Dad, too, before he got strange. They said your dad was the best Kludd they ever had at the big klonvocations. It must have been real hard to have him go like that.

GEORGE: Jdark, he said, and croaked.

JUDY: What?

GEORGE: At the hospital. That's what he said. Jdark, and then he rolled over and died. Terminal furball. Furball in the windpipe.

JUDY: Oh, that sounds awful.

GEORGE: I meant tail pipe. There was this furball that somehow got lodged in the tail pipe of his Ranchero. Did something bad to the whatchamacallit. The throttle spring thing got sprung, got wedged, somehow, on full. Brakes locked, spun out. He could've put the clutch in, but he didn't. Stubborn cuss. Took the steep hill up by Route Seven at fifty-five. Old Pancake Road up by Sandman's Creek. He made the first turn, witnesses say, somehow. No one ever did it that fast before. That's what they say.

JUDY: He must've been quite a man.

GEORGE: He went into the hairpin turn on top of Old Boabdil at seventy. Took out a ninety-year-old oak with him and tore off the edge of Dead Man's Gulch. The drop is about five hundred feet. Into the rapids just beneath the falls. It took them three hours to cut him out of the wreck. He was still alive. They took him to the county hospital, but he wasn't conscious anymore. They called and we got there just in time. He woke up, just before he passed on. Jdark, he said and croaked.

JUDY: That is so tragic, George.

GEORGE: Jdark, he said. That was all.

JUDY: Hold my hand, George.

(They hold hands. Pause.)

JUDY: Life is so mystical sometimes.

(The spying FURBALL *goes away. Blackout)*

Scene Four

(Another night, another parked car. Two FURBALLS *sit in the car, bitching.)*

FURBALL ONE: Shit.

FURBALL TWO: Fuck it.

FURBALL ONE: Shit on you, fuckhead.

FURBALL TWO: Shit on you, why don't you fucking get off my case, you moron.

Mac Wellman 15

FURBALL ONE: Fucking dickbreath is what you are. Fucking monster crapface.

(Pause)

FURBALL TWO: I dunno, this fucking town, this fucking town is driving me crazy. "That's so tragic, George..." "Jdark, he said. That was all..." "Life is so mystical sometimes..."

FURBALL ONE: Fuck, I'd like to fucking fuck all these fucking pussies till they turn puke green and belly up, the stupid fucks.

(Pause. Both FURBALLS *pick their noses.)*

FURBALL TWO: I mean, I really can't stand this fucking place; it's like an itch you can't scratch, a scab that's driving you crazy, or a really gross and disgusting bald spot on the head of somebody you really can't stand; it's kinda like the sort of cheerful, nerdy music they're always playing on public radio: sorta bubbly, sorta goofy, sorta upbeat, you know? But really dead and empty inside. I mean, the whole fucking place rubs my fur the fucking wrong way; I mean, it's all so fucking decent and god-fearing and goody-two-shoes and law-abiding and thankful and smarmy and sentimental and full of wishful thinking and sugar coated bad faith and chintzy, cheesy, boring mediocrity it makes me want to gag. I mean all these totally square fuckheads who only care about God and family and communication and community and law and order and morality and safe sex and global warming and Jesus H Christ and the whole moldy, worn-out crock of shit. It makes me want to spew and leave my lunch all over their well-manicured lawns. I mean, these fucking losers don't have a clue! Fucking smart-ass bigots and liars and cheapskates and schemers and connivers and empty-headed purveyors of the empty hoax of the American dream. I mean, it makes me sick with laughter, all their fake ideals and cant and bullshit and stupid rigmarole and mindless, conventional functional-fixedness, conformity, and lack of spunk. Middlebrow, mainstream, heavy-handed, hypocritical, slimy, rubberized, saccharine, homogenized, namby-pamby, cretinized, dull, repetitive, unavowed, moronic, jerky, overdone, hackneyed, effeminate, creepy, flabby-minded, suburban, knee-jerk, bogus, flatulent, slimeball, cornball, reject, slipshod, uncouth, yahoo, fruitcake, wishy-washy, deaf-and-dumb, bloated, numbskull, puke-faced, flat-footed, goofy, dilapidated, superannuated, depraved, psychotic, pedestrian, rebarbitive, and totally uncool, unhip, and unfun. All of it, deeply insincere. *(He shudders. Pause)*

FURBALL ONE: Who the fuck do you think you are, you fucking meatball? Just look at you! What have you ever done to justify your existence, furface? What makes you think you're so hot? What did you ever accomplish? What right have you got to rant and rail about the cheesy inhabitants of Hillsbottom when you aren't one iota better than them? What new and time-saving machines have you invented? What money have you heaped up and saved through your diligence and industry and perspicacious shrewdness? What new idea has shuddered, stumbled, and lurched forth from the monastic stillness of your furry brain? What histories have you penned, chronicling the hidden purpose behind the vast scenes of horror and pandemonium of human action, scenes hitherto thought meaningless, dark, and inaccessible to the light of reason? What foodstuffs have you planted and hoed, nurtured with your own furry meathooks, through your own furry labors, and by the sweat of your furry brow, and processed, bottled, and crated up for the common good? What beautiful works of art have you imagined in the fiery furnace of your furry, esemplastic imagination, then chopped and hewn out of what hardwood, or cut out of what whole cloth, and polished to a "T," thereby winning cries of wonder and astonishment from crowds of admirers, wherever they assemble, in parks, museums, traffic islands, and in malls and movie theaters? What humble, odious, but high-minded and necessary public service have you rendered, toiling in obscurity, all for the good of others, with no recompense expected or asked for, within the heroic purity of your innermost heart? What joys have you given others, in the form of small gifts or meaningless little gestures of basic human goodwill and positive-mindedness, which might—if only for a moment—lighten the load of those less fortunate than you, those even more bestial and craven, those lost in blind despair within the horrid attics of existence, driven crazy by bats, skunks, and rodents in the insulation and under the floorboards; those whose destiny is other than yours, the overlooked, the undervalued, the unsightly, the woebegone, the mocked and scorned, the deprived, the damned, the doomed, the dead. All of 'em, fuckheads.

FURBALL TWO: No cigar, Furry. The dead don't got no rights.

FURBALL ONE: Don't give me no "No, cigar, Furry." I am more different from you. For I confess that although I am a furball of monster magnitude—a hellacious, badass furball!—I am sincere.

FURBALL TWO: Fuck you, I am bigger than you, and I can whip your furry ass any time I want. I am smarter than you, a better bowler, and will take you on any time at blackjack, craps, or Chinese checkers. I am a better dancer, am more better in bed, a flashier dresser, and have more best-looking shoes than you. I got more important stuff on my mind than you, and do not waste my breath on what is common and low class. My friends are more interesting than your friends, and they are more fun to hang out with. My house is in a more better neighborhood, and your house is a wreck and poorly furnished and I would walk right by without saying "hello" if it were not for wanting to do you a favor on account of you being such a miserable, washed-up, jerkoff, has-been, pathetic loser, and that's a fact. I got more money than you, and have heaped up more valuables, foodstuffs, and loot. My wine cellars overflow with high class swill, and I got whole warehouses of stuff, pretty damn hifalutin' type stuff, stuff the likes of which you never laid eyes on owing to your lack of class, and general cussedness. And what's more I speak my mind more better than you because God love s me and mine better than you and yours and no wonder! because, like, I mean, you ever take a good close look at yourself, man? why, you are *ugly*, and when I say ugly I mean your kind of ugly gives whole new meaning to the higher concept of "ugly"; what's more, I am superior to you in all other respects, and if I have a fault it is that I have lowered myself somewhat by even bothering to associate with one such as yourself, someone whose sense of self-esteem is buried somewhere, somewhere remote, buried butt-up beyond the barbed wire and towers of redemption. A total dickhead.

(The FURBALLS *scowl at each other. Blackout)*

Scene Five

(Another wonderful night, but strange. Two lovers parked in a car. They, too, are dressed in the Klan way. In the bushes a FURBALL *spies upon them.)*

LLOYD: Do you believe that terrible things always have to happen, or not. I mean, if it's possible for some really gross and disgusting event to happen, do you think it has to, or not, which?

TOM: Never really thought about it.

LLOYD: Neither did I, until right now.

TOM: The way I look at it, we must all have a purpose, a purpose that God keeps hidden from us.

LLOYD: How do you mean?

TOM: Well, if God informed us upfront of why we were put on earth there wouldn't be any surprises in it. God must've felt he needed to liven things up, by keeping the true purpose of all of this hidden. Secret, and stuff.

LLOYD: Sometimes, I do wish he had made it a little clearer though. I mean like with car crashes. Child abuse. The divorce rate, and stuff. The sacred and mystical rights of the unborn. Like the plutonium seepage problem near West Hillsbottom, all those people downwind with growths, and how you're not supposed to drink the well water in East Hillsbottom, and stuff.

TOM: That's not been proven.

LLOYD: That's not proven, but it's suspicious. People say it is very likely a big worry.

TOM: It has not been scientifically proven otherwise those in charge of the facility would come out and say so. This is not a case of God's will being murky or his plan for us, it is just a case of the evidence not being all in.

LLOYD: If the evidence were all in, would it make any difference, as far as God's will goes? That's what I mean.

TOM: I don't think so, because nuclear pollution might still be a part of God's design, I mean his plan for Hillsbottom. We might not be able to fathom that plan is all.

LLOYD: Then we're better off not knowing that plan.

TOM: That's a deep thought. I think you have a deep mind, Lloyd.

LLOYD: Tom, I feel so reverent when I think of all the things I don't know, and how majestic the summer sky is at night, and how much God must love us, how much He must have cared all along, millions of years ago, before He had any idea that you or I might exist.

TOM: You know, I've been thinking about you all week.

LLOYD: I didn't think you liked me.

TOM: I told Carol I had a crush on you, and I'd kill her if she told anyone.

LLOYD: I can't believe it. I thought I was the one with the crush.

TOM: I thought you thought I wasn't part of the "in" crowd.

LLOYD: I can't stand those guys. They're such snobs. I can't stand conceited people.

TOM: Neither can I. People who think they're better than you, just because they drive a Corvette their father gave them. Like Ralph.

LLOYD: I can't stand that.

TOM: But you went out with Ralph for six months.

LLOYD: Even then I couldn't stand that about him. First I had a crush on him because I thought he was cute and stuff. But pretty soon I wised up and realized he wasn't sincere. Actually he was a jerk, and just did things to impress his friends. Like Chainsaw and Meatball. Gross. And the furball guy. Whatsisname. Actually I only went out with him because he drove a red Corvette. Red's my favorite color.

TOM: I thought you were madly in love with him.

LLOYD: I wasn't.

TOM: Are you sure?

LLOYD: What are you talking about? You're the one who was making googly eyes all over Susan Hanahan all during the field trip to the...museum. Was it the museum?

TOM: No, it was the nuclear power plant. It was in the cooling unit.

LLOYD: Well, you were the one who * was making eyes at her.

TOM: I was not making eyes at Susan Hanahan. I was only trying to make sure she had someone who could give her the lowdown on who to hang out with. I did not find her attractive. I found her pathetic, actually. but that was before I realized she had this crush on that slob Randolph, can you believe it?

LLOYD: I still cannot believe that. I still cannot believe that anyone could possibly have a crush on someone so nerdy and insincere as Randolph.

TOM: It's bad enough to be nerdy and insincere, but to be nerdy and insincere like Randolph is enough to make a person positively gag.

(Pause)

LLOYD: I have a crush on you.

TOM: I have a monster crush on you.

(They laugh.)

LLOYD: I didn't think anything like this would happen. I just thought you were doing me a favor because my friends aren't as cool as your friends.

TOM: Your friends are just as cool as my friends. I figured you might not go out with me, well, on account of how I don't know anything, and your dad being this famous pervert and all and socially unacceptable and stuff, not that any of it means moosedick to me, hell, my whole family went bankrupt and stuff. We aren't exactly the country club set.

LLOYD: Tom, I don't care what those snobs think. I think you are a very sincere person, and that is the most important to me.

TOM: Really, Lloyd?

LLOYD: Yes, Tom, it is.

TOM: I've never felt this good before.

LLOYD: Neither have I. It's really wonderful. *(Pause)* Do you believe in God, Tom?

TOM: I didn't used to think I did, but when I think about us, and all the terrific feelings I have for you then I think there must be a God, a god who has arranged for everything to work out perfectly, the way it should.

LLOYD: I feel that way too. I feel very sure that you will accomplish wonderful things in your life, Tom, and that you will go to heaven.

TOM: I don't know, Lloyd, sometimes I feel I'm not up to life's challenges.

LLOYD: Hold my hand, Tom.

(They hold hands. Pause)

LLOYD: Life is so mystical sometimes.

(The spying FURBALL *goes away. A long, furry pause)*

LLOYD: So it was you pushed Carol down the well.

TOM: I told Carol I had a crush on you, and I'd kill her if she told anyone.

(Pause)

LLOYD: Tom, you a wicked awful son-of-a-gun.

TOM: Man's got to do what he got to do.

(Pause)

LLOYD: The miracle at Horsedark, ever thought about that?

TOM: You ask me, it was all done with mirrors.

(Pause. LLOYD *takes his hand away.)*

LLOYD: Tom, there's something the matter with you.

(Slow blackout)

Scene Six

(Another nice night, another parked car. The two girls sit in the car, bitching. They've been corrupted by the presence of FURBALLS *in Hillsbottom.)*

JUDY: Molly, do you know why God created the world the way he did? So complicated, I mean?

(Pause)

MOLLY: Shit on you, why don't you fucking get off my case, you moron.

JUDY: Because I've been thinking about it, and I just get more and more puzzled.

MOLLY: Fucking dickbreath is what you are. Fucking monster crapface.

JUDY: Because if there is a divine plan it sure doesn't look it, very divine, that is. Or planlike. It looks kinda like a mess.

MOLLY: Fuck, I'd like to fucking fuck all these fucking pussies till they turn puke green and belly up, the stupid fucks.

JUDY: That's just how I feel. Like I don't know anything. It's really scary. I mean I don't know the name of the state capital. I don't know what my dad does at work. I couldn't name more than two or three South American countries, and I'm not much better when it comes to Europe.

MOLLY: I mean, I really can't stand this fucking place; it's like an itch you can't scratch, a scab that's driving you crazy, or a really gross and disgusting bald spot on the head of somebody you really can't stand.

JUDY: I don't know the difference between good art and bad art. I haven't a clue what a hostile takeover is, nor why junk bonds are junky. I mean why would anybody want them if they're worthless? It doesn't make any sense. I mean the whole fucking place rubs my fur the fucking wrong way. I mean, it's all so fucking decent and god-fearing and goody-two-shoes and law-abiding and thankful and smarmy and sentimental and full of wishful thinking and sugar-coated bad faith and chintzy, cheesy boring mediocrity it makes me want to gag. I mean all these totally square fuckheads who only care about God and family and communication and community and law and order and morality and safe sex and global warming and Jesus H Christ and the whole moldy, wornout crock of shit. It makes me want to spew and leave my lunch all over their well-manicured lawns.

MOLLY: I mean, these fucking losers don't have a clue. Fucking smart-ass bigots and liars.

JUDY: You think they're just pretending?

MOLLY: I think they're all faking it, particularly our parents, our teachers, our social betters, people in positions of authority, and celebrities on T V, and in the halls of Congress, in the churches and klonvocations, and on the radio, even in the middle of the night, when we are all asleep, except Poky the cat. Poky the cat knows. *(Long pause)* Sometimes I wonder if I'm really named Molly, and that freaks me out, because if I am not then who am I, and if I don't have a real name what am I? Maybe I don't exist and this is some kind of a cruel joke your family is playing on me, and I wouldn't put it past them, particularly Dexter, your brother. He says he has a crush on me. But I don't know if Dexter is capable of such a thing, he's such a klutz he couldn't spell I Q if you spotted him the "Q," and he doesn't know much of anything, any more than I do. I know that for a fact.

JUDY: Who the fuck do you think you are, you fucking meatball? Just look at you! What have you ever done to justify your existence, furface? What makes you think you're so hot?

MOLLY: I think the absolute sincerity part of it is the most important, because it's real hard not to know anything unless you are perfectly sincere about it.

JUDY: Sorry.

MOLLY: Judy.

JUDY: Yes. What is it?

MOLLY: What if, maybe, I only think I'm Molly and that in fact I'm Judy and you're Molly and that somehow we got all mixed up, tragically, walking back from school, and Judy... *(A furry pause)* Fuck you, I am bigger than you, and I can whip your furry ass any time I want. I am smarter than you, a better bowler, and will take you on any time at blackjack, craps, or Chinese checkers. I am a better dancer, am more better in bed, a flashier dresser, and have more best-looking shoes than you. I got more important stuff on my mind than you and do not waste my breath on what is common and low class. My friends are more interesting than your friends, and they are more fun to hang out with. My house is in a more better neighborhood, and your house is a wreck and poorly furnished and I would walk right by it without saying hello if it were not for wanting to do you a favor on account of you being such a miserable, washed-up, jerk off, has-been, pathetic loser, and that's a fact. I got more money than you, and have heaped up more valuables, foodstuffs, and loot. My wine cellars overflow with highclass swill, and I got whole warehouses of stuff, pretty damn hifalutin' type stuff, stuff the likes of which you never laid eyes on owing to your lack of class, and general cussedness. And what's more I speak my mind more better than you because God loves me and mine better than you and yours and no wonder! Because, like, I mean, you ever take a good close look at yourself, man? why, you are *ugly*, and when I say ugly I mean your kind of ugly gives whole new meaning to the higher concept of "ugly"; what's more, I am superior to you in all other respects, and if I have a fault it is that I have lowered myself somewhat by even bothering to associate with such as yourself, someone whose sense of self-esteem lies buried somewhere, somewhere remote, buried butt-up beyond the barbed wire and towers of redemption. A total dickhead.

(Pause. The girls look surprised by their little episode of unpleasantness.)

MOLLY: Judy, I think there's something the matter with you.

JUDY: I think there's something strange going on. Something strange is trying to take over Hillsbottom.

MOLLY: But how could that be?

JUDY: We're good people. Good people shouldn't be talking like this. Good people should talk normal. Good people should act sincere.

MOLLY: Judy, I'm afraid.

JUDY: Something bad's gotten into us.

MOLLY: You have to have faith.

JUDY: Faith. *(She looks stunned.)* Yeah.

MOLLY: Judy, I just had a bad thought.

JUDY: I had a bad thought too.

(Blackout)

Scene Seven

(Nice night, just as before. Same old moon, but strange. Bigger and mean-looking. The girl and boy of the first love scene, GEORGE *and* JUDY, *sit in a car. They don't feel so hot.* JESUS *observes them from the tall weeds, hidden.* MELVIN, MOLLY, *and* TOM, *unseen by audience, hide in car.)*

JUDY: I don't feel so hot.

GEORGE: Neither do I.

JUDY: I don't feel so hot, and I think it's your fault.

(A nasty pause. They get out of the car.)

GEORGE: It's not my fault, Judy. You're just pissed because I remind you of Melvin, your previous, jerky, boyfriend. Melvin, who was a total toad, if you ask me, but we aren't the same. * (JUDY *overlaps.)* I am a normal, sweet, good-looking, small-town-type American guy, whereas this Melvin is a true goon, a desperate loser, the kind you wouldn't trust to change a flat tire because he'd be likely to go and do something weird, ** (MELVIN *overlaps)* something uncoordinated, and not put the nuts on right, him being a somewhat alien type of fellow, the artistic type, a member of the glee club, if you get what I mean, a real limp wrist of the first water, and not like me.

*(*MELVIN *climbs up out of the car, and goes after* GEORGE. MOLLY *climbs out after him.)*

JUDY: No, no, no, you got it all wrong, and if I have to explain myself then clearly we have been proceeding along the foggy road of illusion, and there is an absence of trust. And how dare you bring up Melvin, who was kind enough to listen patiently to me when I had my crisis of faith, you probably forget, when Dad kept asking me to dance at the Prom, embarrassing me, us all, so that we had to ask the authorities to take him away to the asylum because of his sudden, twisted sickness; and you paid no attention, and kept jitterbugging with Molly, who you know full well was my best friend, and this when I had my eye on you, and you had your eye on me, at least that's what you said when we got lavaliered two days later, and you took certain liberties, so that I had to admit some fairly unpleasant details of my personal life at confession and Father Greenblast was clearly shocked because he had never heard of such things being done at such a young age, in full knowledge of sin, death, and perpetuity, upon the body of one such as me, innocent, by one such as you, George, clearly a boy of too much experience to say he was normal. So when I lost my faith, that was a premonition of now, and now my soap bubble of hope is burst thanks to you, thanks George, thank you so much. *(She sits down and cries.)*

MELVIN: Well, I am John Q Fedup, and if you ask me I think you're all a bunch of snobs, conceited assholes and, yes, Judy I admit I had this powerful crush on you and, no, I didn't expect nothing from you but you could've, you know, just had the courtesy to return my call, 'cause I know your mom was lying through her teeth when she said you were out, at hockey practice. I mean, I tried being nice, even though it was your Uncles Sedgewick who fired my dad—betcha don't even know that!—at the vee-belt factory in Horsedark, near the county morgue, and that was the beginning of the end for him, he took to drugs and banjo playing with Mrs. Whatshername, the second grade teacher at Horsedark School. I never forgot that, how one of your people did that to one of my people, and it galled me. It heaped me. It's worked me up into a fierce, semicramped state, and my heart wants to barf and blow up. *(Pause)* But I wasn't good enough for you, and you start up with this faggot George creep, this cross-eyed, greasy, Asiatic mongrel, why, his people lived in yurts when my great uncle Williamson Hartbuckle played left guard on the same team as Red Knuckles. Why, he's such a loser he don't even know who Big Red Knuckles is, nor what he done, nor where he growed up, nor what sport he played, nor what his records are, nor which of them are still standing, nor what became of him after the sad accident, nor what his number is that was retired last year in a ceremony up in Horsedark.

MOLLY: How dare you insult me, you whorish slut, who I thought was friend to me when that was clearly an Easter Bunny of mistruth? Do you have moisture on the brain or a growth on the organ of your human reason? You seduced George from me, the turkey, even before we began going out, and you did this out of bitterness and rancor against me because you knew me and my family come of fine, old Aryan stock, and of Eld bended the longbow with the best, in the Black Forest with Hermann and Wolfius and their blond beasts, and our men stand over six feet tall and our genes are strong, like our white, gnashing teeth. *(Pause)* And if we do not dance the hokeypokey it is because we despise the hokepokey and all things common. For we are strong. And furthermore we are more sincere than you, less afflicted with bad thoughts of sex, crime, embezzlement, and bank robbery Thank God.

(She stands, fiercely. Pause. All are suddenly still. All start up together. Loud)

JUDY: What a miserable creep you are, Melvin, * , ** (GEORGE *and* MOLLY *are overlapping*) to bring up this insulting garbage, and who cares what you feel, you and your swinish, low-class family. Why, if I had my way there would be local legislation passed forbidding you and your swinish family from ever spreading your alien, swinish tents and campfires in Hillsbottom. We are a humble, modest people and we do not nose our normal, modest, American noses into other people's lives unless there is the threat of alien contagion, as in your case, which was only prompted by your alien nosing into our ways, which have always been prompted only by the spiritual promptings of our lives, spiritual lives which are far too delicate and intellectually sophisticated for your carnal lips, brains, and feral understanding. You are of the tribe of Belial and Abaddon and must be taught the rule of law. We have tried to teach you this rule of law, but to no avail. You have even spoiled our night of love, here under the magic influence of the summer moon, because you cannot leave be, but must always be tampering with the divine economy of the world, which rules all things, and compels George and me to this spot, to observe our ancient prelapsarian rites, under the furry mantle of heaven. Spite thee, devil! Get thee behind me, Satanist!

GEORGE: Molly, Molly, Molly, for Christ's sake, hear me, I too am of Wotan's mighty crew. Why, therefore, would you not have me when you might've, out back behind the hot dog stand, after we, the Hillsbottom Huns trounced the team from Isle of Hogs, and I could see in your eyes what you wanted, yes, even as your lips denied me, and we were removed from Grace, and expelled into the desert of unsatisfaction and cultural wobble. This, wobbly-legged with lust and lack of satiety, even as the cool night beckoned. *(Pause)* And then you start up with that miserable, slick Norton guy, what a slick, jive-ass he was, no class at all. I mean, what'd he have that I didn't; he didn't have no red Camaro, and he talked funny too, like some abject weirdo from out of state, some abject, suspect, reform school retard from outer space, who didn't have a clue how to be cool. I mean, not a clue. And what the fuck do you want me to do? Wait till the end of time till you put out? I mean, like get serious. *(Pause)* And Judy, you ask. She was strictly a party-time girl, yes, I confess to it, which is why I asked her to go out, event though she is beneath me. Hell, we all know how beneath me she is! So I guess you could say I was dealing with this crippling emotional affliction (which you caused, incidentally), and so where was I to turn, but this scag, Judy, the truly scaggiest of the scaggy. But to her credit she was not too proud, she was not too proud to boff me. Yes, Molly, she boffed me after gym practice, repeatedly, and in the custodian's room during the junior prom, and at the mall, in a dark place, off-limits, near the miniature golf course, and in her room, at her house, and in my room, at our house; and, Molly, I think God would approve this boffing because even though Judy is a dirty, scaggy slut she is sincere, which is more than I can say for you, Molly, yes, you who gave me a hurt that will not heal. Ever.

MOLLY: Wotan, protect me from this horde
 of vicious, hellish, monsterific bipeds
 in sheep's clothing.
May Wotan protect me from these creepy dickheads.
May Wotan bury his steel hatchet in their faces.
May Wotan fry them in his black skillet.
May Wotan howl over their broken limbs.
May Wotan stretch them up the rack,
 over the white-hot coals.
May Wotan rip their impious eyes from their ugly
 heads.
May He chant the sacred mystic syllables of our tribe.
May He prepare oils and greases for the holy jamboree.
May He rattle chains and swing the war club
 to terrify their ancestral spirits.
May He rout their armies and scatter
 the fleeing.
May He show no mercy when it comes to
 extermination.
May His revenge be relentless and exacting.
May He darken the skies with smoke of their
 burning dead.
May He place stones on their bleached bones.
May He curse the dead.
May He melt what is solid.

May He avenge the bad thought.
May He stomp and groan, horribly.
May He roar.
May He piss on their
   dreams.
May He shut his eyes.
May he *(Pause)*
May He do what he must do.
May he fuck them in the head
   till they die. Amen.

(A furry pause. TOM *appears from out of the car.)*

TOM: Well, that's it. I guess none of you are really my friends after all. I plumb well knowed and misknowed all along, yup, cause if'n I were wrong you all woulda been more kindly roundabout here like most, and not up and be all so goshdarn high and mighty 'cause I never done a bad thing to none of you either and if the good Lord would hear me He would take you all up with one hand and fling you down with the other, and stomp on you good with him big furry feet, splat like that, till you were all one big red splotch, 'cause none of you ain't half as sincere as I used to was. So there. Good riddance.

(JESUS *appears with her heavy suitcase.)*

JUDY & MOLLY: *(Singing)*
I sing because I'm happy.
   I sing because I'm free.
For His eye is on the sparrow,
   and I know He's watching me.

(Blackout)

Scene Eight

(JESUS *speaks to the company, assembled at her feet like spokes of a wheel, including the* FURBALLS.)

JESUS: Do you think I came here to reconcile you, brother to sister, father to son, mother to mother-in-law, second cousin twice-removed to step-aunt from out of state, Cincinnati maybe? Furball to furball? Shit-ass no! I came here to raise badass, obstreperous, antisocial, pestiferous, brutalitarian, loudmouthed and chaotic bloody hell. The roaring kind! You swinish, mealy-mouthed bunch of hypocrites wouldn't know the Lord God of Hosts if he swope down and bit you on the ass. All you care about is what you look like, what you look like in a mirror, a mirror some monster furball dreamt up for you to look at to make you blind. America, you got your eyes open so wide you can't see a fucking thing. America, you're crazy if you think your limpdick, milksop, harebrained Christianity has anything whatsoever to do with Jesus H Christ, because that's who's standing here before you in the dusty ruination of the open road, because the whole point of what I am about is to shake up belief, to shake up belief and make people stop being so gosh-darned pleased with theyselves, and take a good look at what a sorry place this world is, what with all the jive-ass bullslinging and endless justifying. And mudslinging. And monumental cheapness of heart and moral stinginess. Furthermore, whosoever puts words in my mouth concerning they fears of the so-called cabal of international faggotry, the scourge of the children of Ham, and the Hebrew contagion— (*With irony*) different folks who ought to be viewed with a skeptical eye as total washouts at maintaining correck social decorum and avoidance of the misnormal—all those who puts words in my mouth concerning these things I have no use for. What the fuck do I care who fucks with who? They fucking is they own concern, and may they use it wisely, and well. Furthermore, whosoever puts words in my mouth, he too fucks with me in the abstrack sense; therefore, I do not like him, because...because, you go figure: If'n I, Jesus H. Christ, had any desire to speak your language, the debased patois of late capitalism, I woulda done so roundabout here likemost, right from the start; but I didn't, so I don't; I won't give you the satisfaction. Because I got nothing to say to you, America. America, I have nothing to say. I prefer the language of furballs, although they are a wicked awful bunch, and spirits of negation, and the mere sight of 'em like to make my skin crawl. I prefer their language because you so much despise it. No, all I wanted, pure and simple, was to create a context for something powerfully human, great, and beautiful, it being the state of nature to leave off with telling who to do what, X in the name of Y, for no other reason than general cussedness. The door opens on your side, I always say—I can't open it! I mean, the handle's on your side and if you don't want to see that, tough shit, it's your problem and none of mine. Face it, you a sleazy, lying, conniving bunch of dickheads. if you fuck up, it's your fault, not mine. And if I had to do it all over again, I'd give the whole matter serious thought. Because of doubts I now possess about the entire enterprise. Because, you know what I got in this bag, do you? *(Pause)* I mean, do you know what this load is which I have chosen to lug with me all down through the ages through the peaks and canyons of oblivion, up to now, do you?

GEORGE: Nope. *

JUDY: No, we don't, ma'am.

JESUS: OF COURSE YOU DON'T, DICKHEADS. BECAUSE you lack imagination, wit, manners, and any sense of humor. *(Pause)* Because anything simple and decent escapes you. *(Pause)* Because you get lost in insane manias that devolve into nightmares of control, slaughter, rapine, and nontemporal unaccountability. You get lost in dumb-ass things like sincerity and infinite regress. Sincerity!? I'll tell you about sincerity! It's not about hooting and hollering. It's about the stillness after all the hooting and hollering has stopped. *(Pause)* WHAT THE FUCK DO I CARE ABOUT YOUR FUCKING SINCERITY?! You can go shove your fucking sincerity up your tail pipe. *(Pause)* In here is the quietest poem ever written. And it is heavy. It is really, really heavy. You *(To* GEORGE*)*, you meathead, yes you, you want to try to pick it up? *(Pause)* Go on. Just try. Pick it up.

(GEORGE *tries and can't do it.*)

JESUS: I am Jesus H Christ *and* I am Jane Q Fedup. *(Pause)* When your time comes, you too, each one, will cry out, "jdark," and be gone. You're looking for the wrong event, that's what you're looking for. *(Picks up the suitcase)* Wake up to the hollow time that is, because that's where your parlous asses are, each and every one. *(She goes. Long pause)*

MOLLY: The Lord giveth and the Lord taketh away.

TOM: Who was that African-American babe?

(Blackout)

END OF PLAY